Wilmington

THE CITY AND BEYOND

Wilmington
THE CITY AND BEYOND

Photography by Mike Biggs/Text by Dr. Barbara Benson

Designed by Bernard Ben Pearce

PUBLISHED BY THE JARED COMPANY
WILMINGTON, DELAWARE

Wilmington—The City and Beyond illustrates the spirit and soul of New Castle County with its splendid photographs of our beautiful cities, quaint towns, and colorful farm areas. This pictorial book reveals the variety and charm of a community established by a fine heritage and outstanding pride.

Dennis E. Greenhouse

Dennis E. Greenhouse
County Executive

THE JARED COMPANY
833 Locust St.
P.O. Box 1948
Wilmington, Delaware 19899

PHOTOGRAPHER: Michael Biggs
PUBLISHER: Alisa Joy Dadone
TEXT: Barbara Benson
DESIGN DIRECTOR: B. Ben Pearce
Photo processing courtesy of Delmar Photo

Published 1991
Printed and bound in Hong Kong
Library of Congress Catalog Card Number 90-5152
ISBN 0-89802-562-1

First Edition: 1991

It is with great pleasure that I invite you to enjoy this pictorial book, *Wilmington—The City and Beyond*, outlining the city of Wilmington's growth over the years. As mayor of the city of Wilmington, I congratulate the many creative individuals responsible for compiling such an exquisite and picturesque history of the First City in the First State.

Daniel S. Frawley

Daniel S. Frawley
Mayor

I am very grateful to a number of people who made this book possible. Maxim Dadone, the force behind the project. Dr. Barbara Benson, who took time from her busy schedule to provide the historical text. Ben Pearce, whose guidance lead us through the book design.

To the many people who provided me access to the churches, museums, and other historic sites, your contributions were invaluable.

Contents

This book is dedicated to my wife Susie and daughter Jill for their love and inspiration.

Introduction

HOW many times have you heard someone say, "Yes, I've seen Wilmington," meaning a blurred view from a speeding car on Interstate 95 or a restricted vision of a railroad-car window. Even those who live in the suburbs often think of Wilmington as only the stop-and-go route they take to and from their store or office. Yet Wilmington is a lively city with a great variety of architecture reflecting a rich heritage. Many of its most photogenic churches, monuments, office buildings, and neighborhood treasures have been captured by Michael Biggs for this book. These photographs provide a visual record of the old and the new, urban development and green spaces, business and domestic life—all juxtaposed within the area outlined by three rivers: the Delaware, the Christina, and the Brandywine.

The Delaware, the Christina, and the Brandywine played a major role in Wilmington's early history. For centuries the area around the three rivers provided a hospitable environment for the peace-loving Lenni Lenape Indians. In the seventeenth century, the fertile soil, lush vegetation, and abundant fish and animals that were so important to the Indians attracted the notice of Europeans in search of new-world riches. Two small Swedish ships, the *Kalmar Nyckel* and the *Vogel Grip*, sailed up the Delaware and into the Christina in March 1638. Dropping anchor at a natural outcropping of rock, they changed forever the way of life along the rivers.

From its base at Fort Christina, the New Sweden colony spread thinly along the Del-

aware. Always underpopulated, the colony lasted less than twenty years. But many Swedish and Finnish settlers remained after the colony ceased to exist, and in 1698 their descendants built Holy Trinity (Old Swedes) Church. The church, the oldest building in Wilmington still standing, conveys the strong sense of permanence of a people who had adapted their old-world traditions to fit a new environment.

Another house of worship, the Quaker Meetinghouse at West Street between Fourth and Fifth (the third meeting on that site), provides a visible reminder of the settlers who built the commercial town of Wilmington a hundred years after the arrival of the Swedish and Finnish colonists. Enterprising settlers from the British Isles, the Quakers saw the potential of Wilmington's location, with the Brandywine offering limitless waterpower and the Christina a port for the building and docking of ships. Beginning in the 1740s Quaker millers began to build flour mills along the Brandywine near what is now Market Street Bridge. The Quakers had judged rightly, for by the time of the American Revolution their mills operated at full capacity, producing a flour of international reputation, Brandywine Superfine.

After the war Wilmington continued to grow. By the end of the eighteenth century, city fathers believed it was time to create a public building that would reflect not just past successes but also faith in the future. The result was Town Hall, located on Market Street between Fifth and Sixth and now a museum owned by the Historical Society of

Delaware. Begun in 1798, just a hundred years after Old Swedes Church, Town Hall reflected a new sophistication in local architecture befitting a prospering, maturing borough. Town Hall looked out upon blocks of brick houses and shops, unpaved streets full of horses pulling wagons and carriages, wharves filled with sailing ships, and the hustle and bustle of people going about their daily lives.

Town Hall marked Wilmington's height as a milling center and port. It soon became clear that the town's continued prosperity depended upon meeting new economic challenges. In the first half of the nineteenth century America experienced a second revolution—a revolution of technology and industry. Steam replaced water in powering equipment, and the railroad replaced the horse and wagon in transporting goods over long distances. For Wilmington this second revolution meant a shift in industrial focus from the Brandywine River to the Christina River. The railroad came to Wilmington in 1837, connecting it with Philadelphia, Baltimore, and a wider economic network. If Town Hall was the capstone of eighteenth-century development, then the railroad station and the train tracks stand as the symbol of Wilmington in the nineteenth century. The train station at Martin Luther King, Jr., Boulevard between Walnut and French streets is the third station on that location, and the route of the original rail line has remained unaltered.

The railroad ushered in a second period of prosperity for Wilmington. Factories—first small and then large—were built along the Christina near the railroad line. Those factories turned out, among other things, railroad cars and equipment, steam engines, machinery, and riverboats for national and international markets. The products of Wilmington's factories could be found in such exotic locations as the subways of Paris, the rivers of Brazil, and the mountains of China. Many of those factory buildings still exist along the Christina, most sadly decaying shells but still reminders of the era of Wilmington's industrial greatness.

With new industries came the need for more workers. Men, white and black, were drawn to Wilmington from the surrounding countryside of Pennsylvania and the Delmarva Peninsula, but the growing factories still needed more hands. Immigrants from Europe came in increasing numbers to work in those factories and for the railroad. Some brought skills but most brought only their strength and a willingness to work hard. They helped build the Wilmington we know today, enriching it through the introduction of their traditions, their food customs, and their community buildings. Their churches and synagogues stood as centers of spiritual worship and community fellowship. Just as Old Swedes provides a tangible legacy of Delaware's first immigrants, such later churches as Saint Hedwig's and Saint Anthony's stand as a link to the immigrants of later centuries.

As Wilmington's population increased, so too did its geographic size. During the second half of the nineteenth century the city expanded in all directions. Trolley lines allowed the more affluent to move to larger dwellings located on the high ground along Delaware Avenue; the less wealthy could move to new neighborhoods of neatly constructed rowhouses. Market Street remained the business and commercial heart of the city. Center city's most architecturally striking building of the late nineteenth century was the Grand Opera House, built in 1871 in the then popular Second Empire style. The Grand survived years of neglect before being restored to its original glory in the 1970s.

By the late nineteenth century, factories such as the Bancroft textile mills and the Du Pont gunpowder mills still made use of the waterpower of the Brandywine, but increasingly the Brandywine area came to be appreciated for its natural beauty. The beginnings of the series of riverside parks and playgrounds that Wilmingtonians enjoy today came through the generosity of William P. Bancroft, who donated eight acres along the Brandywine to the city. By 1990 the city could boast of a series of parks, public pools, and a small zoo. The most beloved symbol of the city's park system remains Rockford Water Tower, one of America's most beautiful water-storage tanks. The city's parks also serve as a reminder of Howard Pyle and the Brandywine School of Painters, for many of their works of art reflect the influence of the natural environment and rustic scenes of northern New Castle County.

In 1903 the Du Pont Company decided to move its corporate headquarters from the banks of the Brandywine at Hagley to a new location in either New York City or Wilmington. Their final choice proved to be the decisive factor in the history of modern Wilmington, enabling it to make the transition from an industrial city to a modern corporate city. The Du Pont Company's new large and impressive office high rise in downtown Wilmington encouraged the rebuilding of the surrounding neighborhood and the creation of Rodney Square. The square was designed in the early 1920s and completed the following decade. The remaining structures surrounding Rodney Square—the City

County Building, the Wilmington Institute Free Library, and the United States Post Office (now the Wilmington Trust) used elements of classical architecture to create aesthetic harmony and to express the growing city's civic pride.

In common with other American cities, the period following World War II did not prove to be an easy one for Wilmington. The city's leaders faced the problem of aging houses, narrow streets, and a changing population. As the trolley gave way to the automobile, the rowhouse to the suburban house with attached garage, and the small grocery store to the supermarket, the city became a less desirable place in which to live and to work.

But Wilmington remained a city with much to offer, and its role as a corporate center continued to expand. The major office buildings of the 1980s reflect the most recent wave of economic development and set the direction of the city as it approaches the twenty-first century. The Brandywine and the Christina still play a role in Wilmington's economy, this time as gateways of urban business renaissance.

Wilmington has grown and changed over time, but it remains an accessible city with neighborhoods of ethnic and architectural distinctiveness. Its monuments and historic buildings commemorate the past, while new office and apartment high rises point toward the future. Those who look around, as Michael Biggs has done, will see the wonders of Wilmington and beyond.

Barbara Benson

Historic Treasures

*R*IGHT, *Holy Trinity Church, popularly known as Old Swede's, dates back to 1698, making it the oldest surviving building in Wilmington. Begun as a Swedish Lutheran church, its ownership was transferred to the Episcopal church in 1792 when there were no longer enough Swedish-speaking members to support a minister from Sweden. The church is located at Sixth and Church streets. Its exterior shows the original walls of Brandywine granite with the brick-and-wood belltower added in 1802. Above, inside the church, the black-walnut pulpit, dating from the church's earliest days, dominates the simple altar and box pews.*

*T*HE State of Delaware created Fort Christina State Park to celebrate the three hundredth anniversary of the landing of the Swedes in America in 1938. Right, a black-granite monument topped by the ship Kalmar Nyckel dominates the park. Created by noted Swedish sculptor Carl Milles, the statue was a gift from the people of Sweden. The relief detail shown here features the meeting of the first colonists with the Lenni Lenape Indians. Above, this log cabin was moved from its original site near Price's Corner to Fort Christina Park to remind visitors that the settlers of the New Sweden Colony introduced log house construction into America.

*R*IGHT, *the Hercules Building with its dramatic design combining granite and glass stands as the centerpiece of Wilmington's Brandywine Gateway development of the 1980s. Above, a statue has been placed in the park between the Hercules Building and the Brandywine River, where the H. Fletcher Brown High School once stood. Sculpted by Charles C. Parks and entitled "The Apprentice," the statue honors Brown for his support of vocational education.*

THIS beautifully simple building overlooks the Brandywine from its location at the foot of West Street. Built in 1740 as Wilmington's first Presbyterian church, the building was moved from its original location at Tenth and Market streets in 1922 to make way for the Wilmington Institute Free Library. The building is now the home of the Colonial Dames of America in the State of Delaware.

*I*N *the photo right, the Market Street side of the Du Pont Company's corporate
headquarters in downtown Wilmington seems to loom above the Caesar Rodney
Equestrian Statue in Rodney Square. Constructed in sections beginning in 1906, the
building contains offices, an hotel, a theater, a bank, and small shops. Above, sculptor
James Edward Kelly commemorated Rodney's famous ride to Philadelphia to vote for
independence in 1776 by showing the patriot sitting proudly astride a horse in full gallop.
The statue and the square date to the 1920s.*

*R*IGHT, *looking south to the Tenth-Street side of Rodney Square, the Delaware Trust building rises above the statue. Alfred I. du Pont built the building following a bitter business split with his cousin Pierre. The modern high-rise tower was added in the 1950s. The Wilmington Institute Free Library fronts on Rodney Square but is hidden by the trees. Built in 1922-23, the library, with its Greek frieze and columns, shown in a detail, above, appears as a temple of knowledge.*

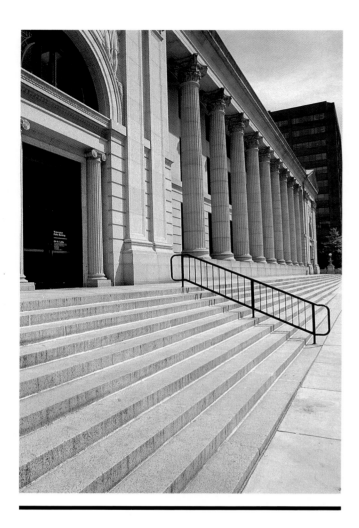

*A*BOVE, *the Public Building, completed in 1917, serves as the anchor for the east side of Rodney Square. Designed in a style evoking classical grandeur, then popular for public buildings throughout the United States, the facility provided space for both city and county government, replacing both Town Hall and the courthouse torn down to make way for Rodney Square. Right, the Wilmington Trust Center on the north side of Rodney Square combines two periods of twentieth-century architecture. A modern office tower rises out of the old 1930s federal building with its richly ornamented facade dominated by the spread-winged eagle over the door.*

GRACE Methodist Church, at Ninth and West streets, was built in 1865 to celebrate the first century of Methodism in Wilmington and the Union victory at Gettysburg, which saved the city from the possibility of invasion by Confederate troops. The exterior view, right, shows the Gothic style of the church, with its distinctive green serpentine stone supplied from quarries in nearby Chester County, Pennsylvania. The interior, shown above looking toward the choir loft, reflects the simple yet expansive nature of what was then the largest church in the city.

*T*HE *Friends Meeting located at Fourth and West streets was completed in 1817, the third meeting on Quaker Hill. A burial ground surrounds the unadorned brick structure. Many of Wilmington's leading citizens are buried there, including John Dickinson, a signer of the Constitution, and Thomas Garrett, the famous abolitionist.*

THE crown jewel of nineteenth-century Wilmington was the Grand Opera House on Market Street, constructed in the early 1870s. Above, the building's cast-iron exterior topped by a Mansard roof illustrates the exuberance of the then-popular Second Empire style. There is a masonic symbol in the pediment above the doorway. The Masonic Order built the Grand Opera House to provide meeting rooms for themselves as well as a large commercial theater for the city. Both the exterior and the opulent interior, right, were restored to their original glory in the 1970s. With its elaborately decorated ceiling and stage, the Grand Opera House recalls the decorative flourishes of the Victorian era.

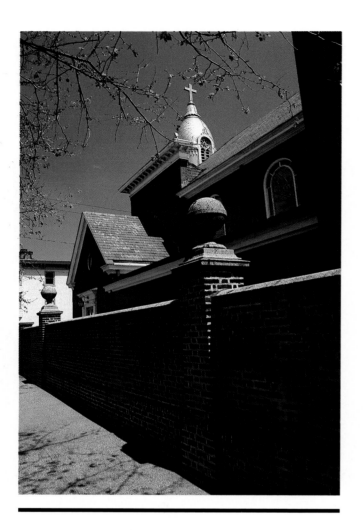

SAINT Peter's Cathedral, above, is the oldest Roman Catholic church in Wilmington. Built at Sixth and West streets in 1816, the church has been the seat of the Bishop of Wilmington since 1868. Saint Peter's has been expanded and altered a number of times over the years. The beautifully restored interior, right, features stained-glass windows, coffered ceiling, and rounded archways.

THE Historical Society of Delaware's Willingtown Square is an enclave of six historic houses, located in the 500 block of Market Street. Moved to the site in the mid 1970s to save them from demolition, these houses are precious remnants of the architecture of Wilmington in the late eighteenth and early nineteenth centuries.

*A*BOVE, *Wilmington's Town Hall, begun in 1798, remained the seat of city government until 1917. An elegant Federal-style building, located on Market Street between Fifth and Sixth, Old Town Hall expresses the pride and civic consciousness of early Wilmingtonians. It is now a museum of the Historical Society of Delaware. Right, the cupola served more than a decorative function: it was used to watch for fires that could break out and quickly destroy large parts of a closely built city.*

THIS aerial view captures Wilmington looking from the southeast. In the foreground are the Christina River, the railroad station, and the new high rises that form the Christina Gateway. New construction in many architectural styles testifies to the city's corporate expansion in the 1970s and '80s. Today the city mixes old with new, office towers with small stores and row houses.

RIGHT, the Christina Gateway features new office buildings, such as 3 Christina Center at Walnut and Second streets, and unique public spaces, like this sculpture garden that uses modern building materials to evoke the architecture of the past. Above, 1 Christina Center provides the backdrop for miniature sculpted city servants, including policemen and firemen, that decorate the entrance to the William T. McLaughlin Public Safety Building on Walnut Street at Fourth.

W*ILMINGTON'S train station has been a city landmark since its construction in 1906 by the Pennsylvania Railroad. Right, designed by the noted Philadelphia firm of Furness, Evans and Company in the Romanesque style, the brick and terra-cotta building is topped by a clock tower. Above, the modern mosaic in the entryway on French Street dates from the most recent restoration of the station in the 1980s.*

*R*IGHT, *a close-up view of the sculpture entitled "Father and son" captures the realistic detail characteristic of the work of the renowned local sculptor Charles C. Parks. The statue honors Peter Spencer and stands in Spencer Plaza on French Street between Eighth and Ninth close to the site of the Mother African Union Methodist Church which Peter Spencer began in 1812. Visitors to Spencer Plaza can also see a plaque, above, commemorating the Underground Railroad and two of its brave leaders: Thomas Garrett, a businessman and abolitionist, and Harriet Tubman, an escaped slave who led other slaves to freedom.*

THESE two memorials to soldiers lost in war stand in Brandywine Park on opposite sides of Baynard Boulevard. Above, the Todd Memorial, dedicated in 1925, honors Delaware soldiers and sailors who died in World War I. The monument features a bronze Winged Victory with uplifted arm. Right, the memorial to those killed or missing in action in the Vietnam War consists of a base with tablets of names topped by the poignant statue of two soldiers, one dead and one alive.

WIMINGTON'S *Park Plaza condominium tower rises through the Japanese cherry trees of Josephine Gardens, located on the north side of Brandywine Park at Van Buren Street. These beautiful trees have graced the park since 1933, when Colonel J. Ernest Smith presented them to the city in memory of his wife, Josephine Tatnall Smith.*

*L*ED *by Father John Francis Tucker, the leaders of Wilmington's Italian community built Saint Anthony of Padua Church in 1925-26. Right, an exterior view of this Roman Catholic Church, located at Du Pont and Ninth streets, shows a design reminiscent of the church architecture of the parishioners' native land. The round rose window, artwork, and rich ornamentation seen in the interior view, above, are but a few of the details expertly executed by craftsmen from the Italian community.*

RIGHT, Admiral Samuel Francis Du Pont looks out from his post at the Tower Road entrance to Rockford Park. This statue of the hero of the Battle of Port Royal in the Civil War stood in Du Pont Circle in Washington, D.C., from 1884 until 1920, when it was moved to Wilmington, Du Pont's hometown. In this view, the admiral appears to be standing watch over the water tower. Above, a detail of the water tower in Rockford Park, built in 1899-1901, shows the closed-in observation deck and the granite exterior that turn a functional public work into an aesthetic treasure.

*R*IGHT, *the Delaware Art Museum on Kentmere Parkway was constructed in the 1930s to house works of Wilmington native Howard Pyle and Samuel Bancroft's world-renowned collection of English Pre-Raphaelite artists. The most recent addition to the building in 1987 provides space for the museum's expanding collections and for changing exhibitions. Above, this interior view of a gallery shows a number of works by Pyle, known as the father of the Brandywine tradition in American art.*

ABOVE, the integrated collection of buildings that make up the Episcopal Cathedral Church of Saint John recalls English medieval church architecture. John Notman, the noted Scottish-born American architect, designed the church and spire in 1857; the other buildings and cloister are twentieth-century additions. The cathedral replaced a notorious tavern at the corner of North Market Street and Concord Avenue. Right, the dramatically displayed pipe organ and dark-wood hammer-beam ceiling continue the English medieval theme in the interior.

*W*ALKER'S *Mill, right, and Breck's Mill, above, stand as reminders of the importance of the waterpower of the Brandywine in the nineteenth century. The two mills, located just below the mills at Hagley, were built between 1810 and 1813 to produce cotton cloth and have been used for a variety of purposes over the years. They are preserved today as part of the Hagley Museum.*

THE tranquil beauty of a spring day at the Hagley Museum can almost make one forget the importance of the site to American industrial history. The mill buildings in the background once used the waterpower of the Brandywine to produce gunpowder at the Du Pont Company's first powderyards. Today the Hagley Museum uses these preserved mills to interpret this early period of American industry.

*R*IGHT, *Christ Church, Christiana Hundred, sits amid ancient trees on a hilltop overlooking the Brandywine. It was built in the mid-1850s to serve Du Pont Company powder mill workers and owners alike. Above, the chapel, located in an adjacent building, strongly suggests the English antecedents of the Episcopal church.*

VISITORS to the Winterthur Museum and Gardens can enjoy the many acres of flowers, shrubs, and trees developed by Henry F. du Pont in the early twentieth century. The gardens of Winterthur, located in the rolling hills north of Wilmington, provide a beautiful setting for du Pont's incomparable collection of American decorative arts.

ROCKWOOD *Museum, right, was originally the Wilmington home of Joseph Shipley,
Quaker merchant-banker. Shipley built the house in 1851 in the Rural Gothic style that he
had come to admire while living in Great Britain. Fine grounds surround the house. The
interior view of Rockwood, above, shows the reception room, dominated by a portrait of
Effie Bringhurst Goldsmith dressed as the queen of Lorraine for a costume ball.*

LOCATED just north of Wilmington on Philadelphia Pike, Bellevue was the home of William du Pont from 1928 to 1965. Du Pont altered the house, built in 1850, to look like Montpelier, James Madison's house in Virginia. The house is now part of Bellevue State Park.

SURROUNDED by 300 acres of woods and gardens, Nemours Mansion on Rockland Road, right, brings a sense of old France to the Brandywine. Alfred I. du Pont built this splendid house in 1909-10 to resemble a Louis XVI chateau and named it Nemours in honor of his ancestral home in France. Above, the gardens of Nemours also reflect the French influence through the use of formal flowerbeds, shrubbery, sculpture, and fountains.

Landscapes

WILMINGTON'S past and present are reflected in this peaceful winterscape along the Brandywine River.

AZALEAS and dogwoods announce the coming of spring along the millrace at the Hagley Museum.

A kaleidoscope of autumn colors illuminate the sun drenched waters near Wilmington's Josephine Gardens.

*L*ATE *afternoon sunlight sets daffodils aglow on the hillsides of Valley Garden Park.*

*N*EW *fallen snow and ice transform Hoopes Reservoir into a winter wonderland.*

RUNNERS stride along the swift flowing waters of the Brandywine River near the start of the annual Caesar Rodney Half Marathon.

WATERFOWL find refuge in the peaceful waters of Bellevue State Park on a foggy November morning.

A late winter snowstorm deposits a velvet like blanket over the flowering trees of Josephine Gardens.

*S*HADES *of yellow and green paint the banks of Red Clay Creek west of Wilmington.*

SLEDDERS frolic on the hills of Wilmington's Rockford Park.

ACRES of wildflowers transform the grounds of the Nemours Mansion into a cavalcade of color.

THE morning sun radiates through the multicolored foliage on the grounds of Wilmington's Banning Park.

A solitary Canada goose rests on the waters of the Brandywine River near the Washington Street Bridge.

FERNS and azaleas in the Winterthur Museum woodlands reveal the delicate hues of spring.

AUTUMN unveils its spectacle of colors in northern Delaware's "chateau country."

*M*EMORIES *of winters gone-by come to mind in this time-honored scene at the Hagley Museum.*

*A*N *autumn evening on the Brandywine provides the perfect setting for friends to meet.*

THE grounds of Rockwood Museum beckon the arrival of spring with an unusual display of flora and fauna.

A farm near Centreville offers a picturesque Christmas greeting to travelers on Kennett Pike.

EVENING settles in over Wilmington's business district near the Brandywine Gateway.

BILLOWING clouds and azure skies provide a striking contrast to the autumn foliage at Brandywine Creek State Park.

HORSES bask in the sun near Greenville on a beautiful afternoon in May.

WILMINGTON'S Rockford Park displays a tranquil mood after a February snowfall.

Urban Details

*M*ANUFACTURERS *Hanover Plaza and the Hercules Building give a new urban image to the Brandywine Gateway area.*

A *playful wall mural reflects the ethnic art of Wilmington's Southside.*

*A*NGULAR *planes of sculpture jut into the sky at the Christina Gateway.*

*N*AMES *of fallen heroes appear against the silhouetted soldiers of the Vietnam Memorial.*

James T. Morris, J

Jesse L. Moses

William J. Murphy

William L. Nellans

Frank W. Nelson,

Edmund L. Palczev

Samuel Paoletti

George Edward Pa

Wayman E. Paskin

George F. Perry,

William A. Pollard

Charles E. Porter

Larry F. Potts

Victor E. Press

Thomas John Pro

*B**LUE** skies reflect in the mirrored glass of the Bank of Delaware Building.*

THE center cupola of the Grand Opera House reveals an elaborate display of architectural shapes.

CONTEMPORARY patterns of concrete and glass shape the Manufacturers Hanover Plaza and the Pei Building on Market Street.

*T*RINITY *Episcopal Church stands nobly against the modern structure of the Chase Manhattan Building.*

*L*ATE *afternoon light casts interesting shadows on the textured walls of Willingtown Square.*

About the photographer . . .

Mike Biggs is a graduate of Brandywine High School and the University of Delaware.

He has sold his photographs as wall decor and stock photos for over fifteen years and has had his work published exclusively in Delaware calendars since 1987. Other books of his photography include *Delaware . . . A Photographic Journey* and *The Delaware Seashore.*

Biggs is a counselor at the Stanton Campus of Delaware Technical and Community College and resides with his wife Susie and daughter Jill in Bear, Delaware.

About the author . . .

A native of Illinois, Barbara Benson received degrees from Beloit College and Indiana University. She has been in Delaware since 1973, first at the Hagley Museum and Library, and since 1980, the Historical Society of Delaware, where she is executive director and managing editor of *Delaware History* magazine. Dr. Benson writes and speaks frequently on Delaware history and is active in many historical activities and community organizations.

About the designer . . .

Bernard Ben Pearce is an award-winning graphic designer employed at the Stanton/Wilmington Campus of Delaware Technical & Community College. *Dynamic Graphics of Illinois; the Government of Trinidad Postage Stamp Commission; and Delaware's IABC* are among those who have honored him. In 1988 he won the commission to design and illustrate the 25th Anniversary Civil Rights commemorative historical book, *The Genuine American Music.*

Pearce holds the Bachelor of Fine Arts degree in graphic design from the Columbus College of Art & Design in Ohio and is currently a candidate for the M.A. degree at the University of Baltimore in Maryland.